Published by Moleskine SpA

Images / **Giancarlo Iliprandi**

Texts / **James Victore, Pietro Corraini,
Giancarlo Iliprandi**

Publishing Director / **Roberto Di Puma**

Publishing Coordinator / **Igor Salmi**

Translations / **Steve Piccolo**

Text Editor / **Miranda Popkey**

Graphic Design / **Pietro Corraini**
with **Maria Chiara Zacchi** and **Giulia Semprini**

The Naked Notebooks
is a project by **Pietro Corraini**

ISBN 9788867324866

First edition 2015

Printed in Italy by
CTS Grafica

FSC
www.fsc.org

MIX
Paper from
responsible sources
FSC® C009945

Many thanks to Monica Fumagalli and Carin Goldberg

Sketch,

GIANCARLO

Think,

ILIPRANDI

Draw.

Pietro Corraini

MOLESKINE

The most beautiful thing a human can do is draw a mark with his bare hands. This is the beginning of everything. To feel the urgency to draw, to make a statement and leave a trace of yourself—it's the very first act of man. The joy of pure, authentic human communication is a trait shared over generations. The screevers at Lascaux handed it to Giotto and Hokusai who in turn give it to your children—all the way to you.

In drawing it's impossible to lie, drawing is honesty. To commit to a line to paper, is to reveal your thoughts and reveal some truth about yourself. An artist committing a line to paper—immediate and authentic—is the most personal of acts. You expose yourself in drawing. We now have tools, tablets and apps that try to circumvent the humanity, to cheat the process, but really there is no other way, drawing is truth.

This is what we are priveleged to find in the pages of Giancarlo Iliprandi's sketchbooks. To see the truth, the thoughts, the man in his works straight from his hand. We are allowed to see the process and the artist at play. In these sketches we are witness to tiny decisions made along the way. Jagged little thoughts searching for truth. We see mistakes that become doors to newer ideas. The freedom Iliprandi allows himself in his line is imminently present in his work. Whether it's the human form or the studied geometry of letterforms, there's a freedom in his elegant gestural lines. So often the sketch loses some of it's fervor in the process to finish, but like the drawings of sculptors like David Smith or Henry Moore, we see Iliprandi's elegant and fine lines later turned into bold, graphic and powerful images. The life of the drawing remains fresh and vibrant in GI's work.

Like me, I am sure you will feel some kindred spirit, a sympathetic relationship when you look at Giancarlo's work. I imagine part of the vital machinery of his thoughts includes clutching a pen or pencil. Now, I must get back to my drawings…

James Victore

#1

Sketch,
think,
draw.

Sketch,
think,
draw.

Once, by devoting yourself completely to training, you have learned the techniques perfectly, the action will move through the arms, the legs, and the body, but not the mind; you will no longer be attached to your training, but neither will you oppose yourself to it, and you will be able to execute any technique with dexterity. You won't know where your mind is, and so the demons won't find it either. To reach this state you have to practice. If you train to the best of your abilities, the training vanishes. This is the secret of all the Ways.

Yagyū Munenori, XVII century

13

Browsing through Giancarlo Iliprandi's travel notebooks and chatting with him about deserts and lettering, one wonders, in the end, does the drawing make itself? Digging through Giancarlo Iliprandi's personal archives one finds many, so many, pages of sketches, drawings, drafts. There are papers and bits of research related to his profession as a graphic designer, at a time when the profession had only just arrived in Italy; and then there

Drawing for the Winter Olympics, Turin, 2006

are the eclectic notebooks Iliprandi carried with him on his travels, all different—both notebooks and voyages. At first glance, they appear to come from two different worlds. The eclecticism of these notebooks represents both the pragmatic professional problem solver as well as the passionate artist represented by his instinctive drawing and doodling. But in fact, these are not two different worlds at all, especially not for a graphic designer like Ilpriandi who in his commissioned projects, as in his drawings and texts, seeks a lightness, an incisive quality, that only the synthesis of a well-balanced, well-trained pencil stroke could express.

Cover, *Sci* magazine #64bis, 1966

SCI SPECIALE

SCIATORE

RIVISTA ILLUSTRATA
DI SPORT INVERNALI

OTTOBRE 1966 - N. 64 bis

NUMERO SPECIALE DEDICATO
ALL'EQUIPAGGIAMENTO

SCARPE DA SCI QUALIFICATE SCARPE DA SCI TIPO TURISMO

ATTACCHI BASTONCINI OCCHIALI PORTASCI ALTRI ACCESSORI
SCI PER COMPETIZIONI ALPINE SCI PER TURISMO

SCARPE DA SCI PER DONNA E BAMBINO
SCI PER RAGAZZI SCI PER FONDO

SCARPE PER FONDO E SCI ALPINISMO

IL MERCATO DELLO

Closely observing the pages and sketches of these diaries, we can see the birth of a drawing, therefore we catch a glimpse of the gestures and movements of the hands.

In the silence of the desert, as in the most colorful ceremonies, a few lines and even fewer colors are all one needs in order to *tell a story*. In each sketch Iliprandi is able to condense all the emotions that inspired those strokes. These are true diaries: they are not intended to be resolved drawings or realistic depictions of the panorama, but notes from one point of view, which will later, perhaps, become resolved drawings.

In the notebooks, the author and the subject meet, and drawing vanishes in favor of gesture. On these pages, marks become mountains, a single line made with a ballpoint pen becomes a face; a doodle serves tea. Therefore one never sees the effort that indicates the attempt to make a handsome drawing.

Iliprandi, a great athlete among the graphic artists of his generation, says that drawing is like skiing: taking a nice curve is like tracing a nice line. In skiing, the important thing is the relationship between the skier and the snow. The gesture, apart from the trail it leaves behind, is satisfying, liberating.

Only after having learned to make good lines can you try to draw, for example, a face. And then, even if the face is totally different from reality, the mark left by the pen will be clean. The first step is to equip oneself with

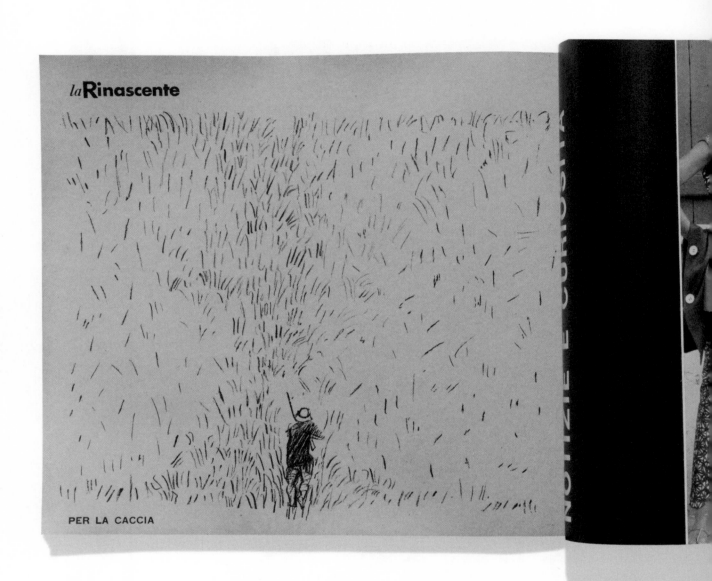

Advertisement for *La Rinascente*, *Sci Nautico* magazine #4, 1960

*la*Rinascente

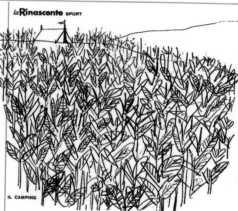

Advertisement for *La Rinascente*, *Sci Nautico* magazine #11-12, 1961

a tool of expression capable of following along with one's thoughts, from moment to moment, over time. That tool will be refined and improved, and its product will come to resemble reality. But the first thing to do is to make sure that one's hand is following along with what one thinks: establishing a dialogue with the hand.

In selecting the best materials for this book, travel memories and drawing tools are a consistent theme. Clearly, Iliprandi likes to experiment, therefore different voyages are narrated using different techniques. Sometimes, the choice is left to happenstance, like the day in Chad when he forgot his watercolors and made line drawings of all the votive statues encountered along the way. Other times, it is the journey itself that decides. "Watercolors are different from drawing, with two different methods, two different times, both connected to technique. What I find interesting about watercolors are the masses, the hues. Drawing, on the other hand, produces a descriptive document."

Iliprandi draws constantly. It not only keeps his hand in shape, but it is a way of continually taking note of the world and, above all, of knowing how to *see*. Faced with a white page, a black line and some protrusions, he says: "When you draw landscapes you have to feel the depth of field. Zooming in and out, like a camera, brings things closer, and pushes them back. You have to have a certain sense of space."

19

Iliprandi continues: "To be able to draw well, you must be humble. Arrogant people cannot draw well: it takes self-criticism."

Before becoming real drawings, the sketches are done over and over, gestures repeated until the right combination is found—one combination useful for an exhibition, perhaps, another for a poster. He often copies and remakes his own drawings. His lines in the notebooks are etched in memory and can be recaptured simply by repeating the same gestures.

"Although I don't rely on photographs and sketches to make my drawings, the experience of taking the photographs and making the sketches is crucial to the relationship I am cultivating with my subjects. If I have images I haven't experienced, I can manage, at best, to make illustrations, but these drawings are cold ones."

This characteristic is a constant in all of Iliprandi's work, in his drawings, writings, posters, logos and books: nothing is ever cold and distant. Because he can enter his subjects and knows how to draw forth their humanity (it makes no difference whether we're talking about a person or a mountain); every sketch, every project, tells a story. Many stories are inside these drawings. Most prominent and compelling of all is the story of Giancarlo Iliprandi.

24

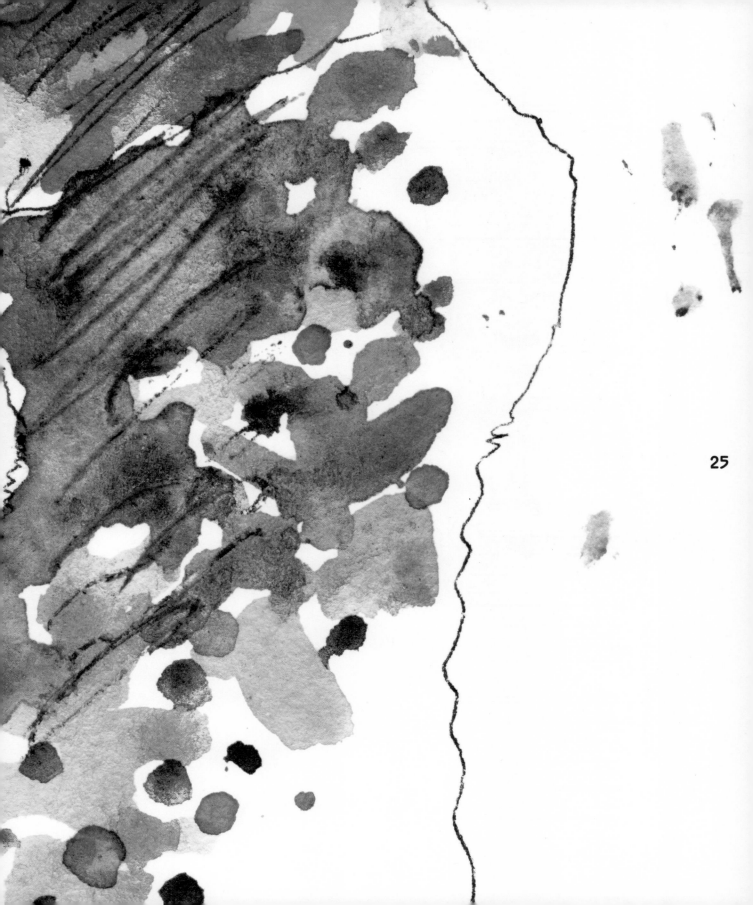

25

26

27

/ The Katyusha *has not finished launching its rockets, which lie all around. The vehicle has been picked clean, they've taken the motor, the wheels, the seats, the weapons, but not the rockets* /

Tutti gli amanti
portano il Turbant.
Per lavorare
la pupillina si copunta
è più elegante

1

GRANDE CERIMONIA FUNEBRE
Cosa portano i portatori? meglio non chiedere

2

1 / All the Omanis wear a turban to work. The embroidered skull-cap is more elegant /
2 / Big funeral ceremony. What are the porters carrying? Better not to ask /

❝ At times it would be better
to stop drawing. **❞**

1 / The mask is that of Batman. They must be "Batmanites" /
2 / These pharaohs have handsome profiles small noses long
eyes space helmets and those sheaths attached to the chin
like improbable beards /

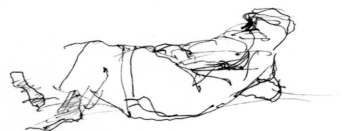

1 CI HANNO DATO UNA GUIDA PER DUE GIORNI. PER
ANDARE A PASSASSA, E RIMEDAR. DORME O PRESA_

34

PARTICOLARI IMPORTANTI
2 ombrellini gialli. Movimenti delle mani. Cietole con offerte e fiori

1 / *They gave us a guide for two days. To go to Fassassa.*
It's Ramadan. He sleeps or prays /
2 / *Important details. Yellow umbrellas. Movements of*
the hands. Bowls with offerings and gifts /

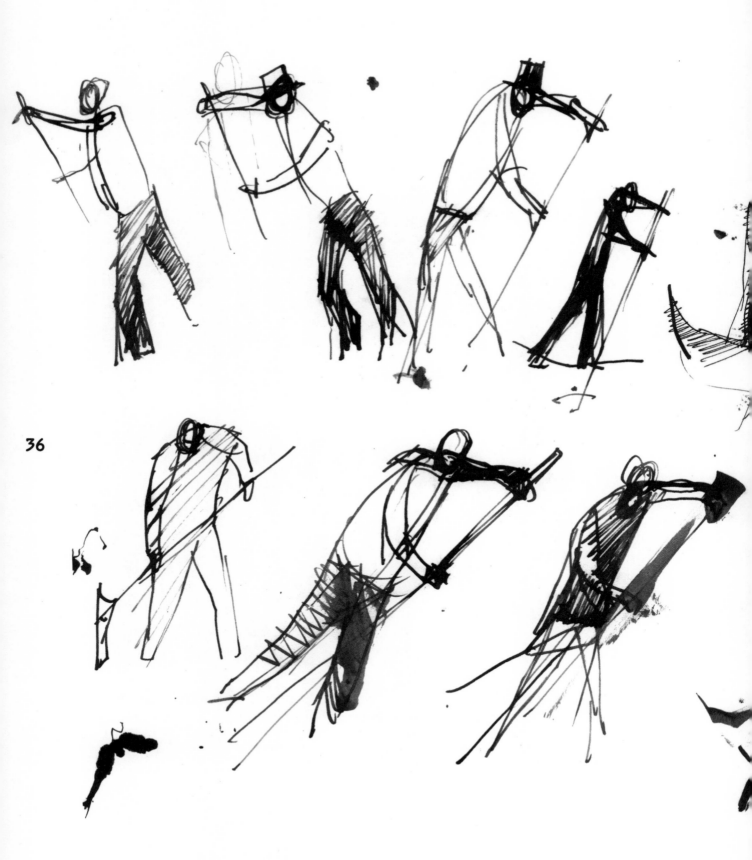

36

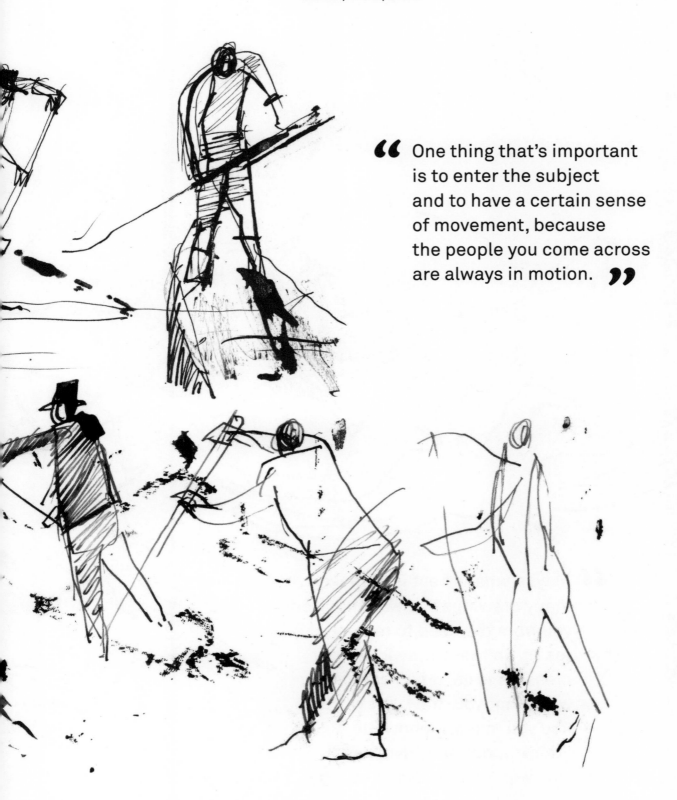

❝ One thing that's important
is to enter the subject
and to have a certain sense
of movement, because
the people you come across
are always in motion. **❞**

37

"Maybe what's best is to make many drawings in a way that frees you from the need to represent reality: in these drawings, your pleasure is no longer connected with what you draw, but with the line you make. Meanwhile, I think about primitive man, who wasn't primitive at all."

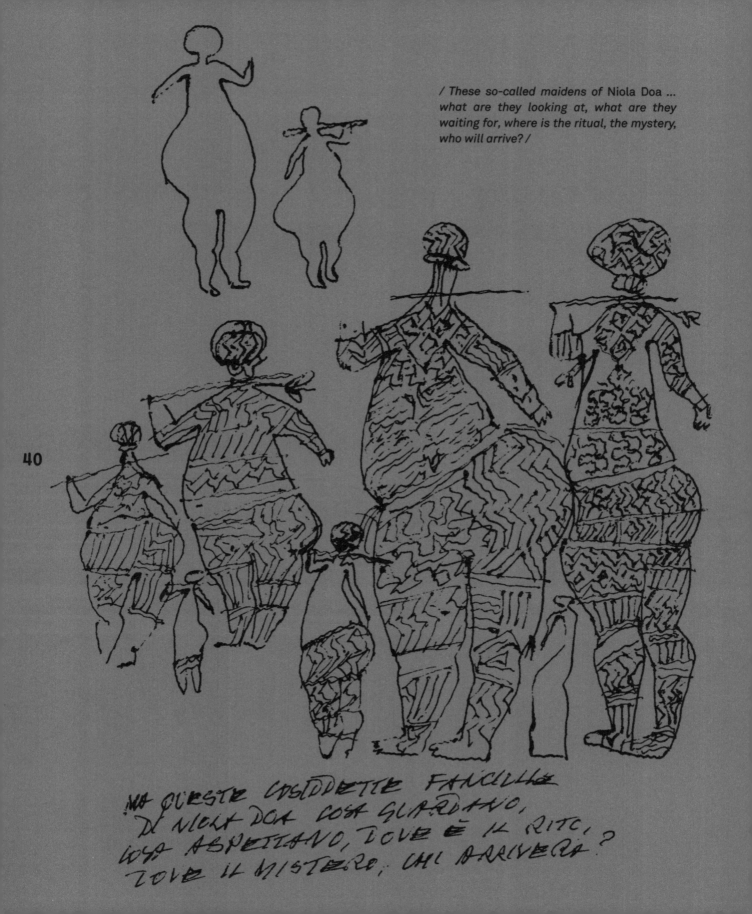

/ These so-called maidens of Niola Doa ...
what are they looking at, what are they
waiting for, where is the ritual, the mystery,
who will arrive? /

40

MA QUESTE COSIDDETTE FANCIULLE
DI NIOLA DOA COSA GUARDANO,
COSA ASPETTANO, DOVE È IL RITO,
DOVE IL MISTERO, CHI ARRIVERÀ?

① ASCIA
TENERIANA

② ASCIA
LEVIGATA

③ ASCIA
A GOLA

④ ASCIA
PERIFOCUM?
O FALLOIDE

1 / tenerean axe
2 / polished axe
3 / grooved axe
4 / phallic axe
5 / arrowheads
6 / leaf-blade spearhead

graffiti incidente

arre famiglia di roccioni.

⑤ PUNTE DI FRECCIA

⑥ PUNTA DI LANCIA
A FOGLIA

42

/ The vendor women appear and disappear in a maze of poles: a forest /

46

/ In the shade of the big portico under the arches you can find anything /

PUNTA ARENAS È UNA CITTADINA INTERESSANTE E VIVACE.
LA PRIMA COSA CHE TI COLPISCE È IL COLORE DI QUESTI TETTI DI LAMIERA,
GRIGIOVERDI, GRIGIOAZZURRO, ROSSI AMARANTO, ROSSI CILIEGIA SINO AL GERANIO
MA IL COLORE DOMINANTE PARE ESSERE IL VERDE IN TUTTI
I SUOI SOTTOTONI - TURCHESE, SMERALDO, BIGLIARDO, POI VERDE PINO,
VERDE VAGONE, VERDE MILITARE, VERDE SALVIA, VERDE MARCIO.
MA QUANTI SONO MAI I TONI DI VERDE CHE RICONOSCI, QUELLI CHE
CHIAMI PER NOME QUELLI CHE CERTI PITTORI HANNO ETERNATO
CON IL LORO NOME COME, AD ESEMPIO IL VERONESE.

PUNTA ARENAS - PATAGONIA   OTTOBRE 1992   ILIPRANDI

Sketch, Think, Draw.

/ Punta Arenas *is an interesting, lively town. The first thing that strikes you is the color of these sheet-metal roofs, gray-green, lead gray, amaranth reds, reds from cherry to geranium, but the main color seems to be green, in all its sub-tones: turquoise, emerald, billiard. Then pine green, wagon green, military green, sage green, sludge green. But how many tones of green can we recognize, those we call by name, those which certain painters have immortalized with their name, like Veronese, for example?* /

LAGO PEHOE. PATAGONIA D'TORRE 1994

51

CIRCO DI ARCHEI – 2 GENNAIO 2011

53

Sketch, Think, Draw.

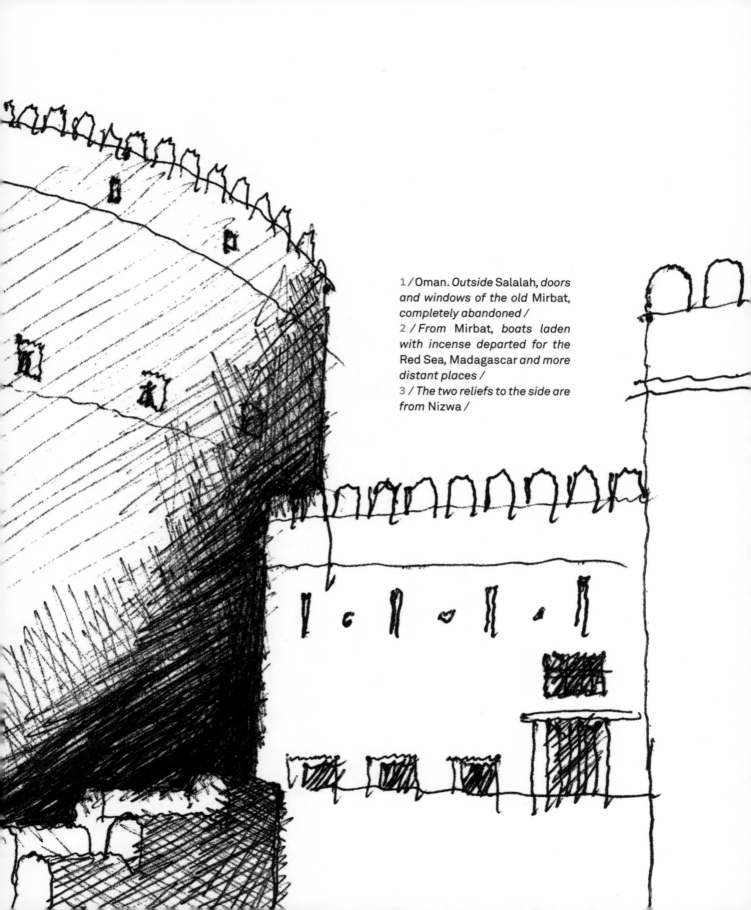

1 / Oman. *Outside* Salalah, *doors and windows of the old Mirbat, completely abandoned /*
2 / *From* Mirbat, *boats laden with incense departed for the* Red Sea, Madagascar *and more distant places /*
3 / *The two reliefs to the side are from* Nizwa /

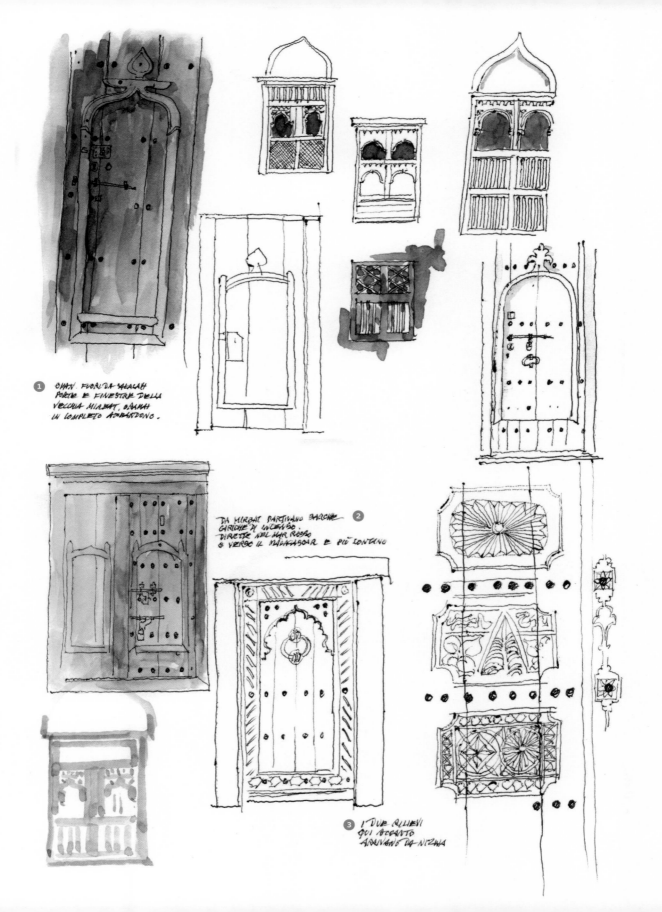

① CHAN. FUORI DA SALALAH
PORTE E FINESTRE DELLA
VECCHIA MIRBAT, OMAN.
IN COMPLETO ABBANDONO.

② DA MIRBAT PARTIVANO BARCHE
CARICHE DI INCENSO.
DIRETTE NEL MAR ROSSO
E VERSO IL MADAGASCAR E PIÙ LONTANO

③ I DUE ALLIEVI
QUI ACCANTO
ARRIVANO DA NIZWA

58

“ I like space, emptiness,

where there is no true end. 🠖🠖

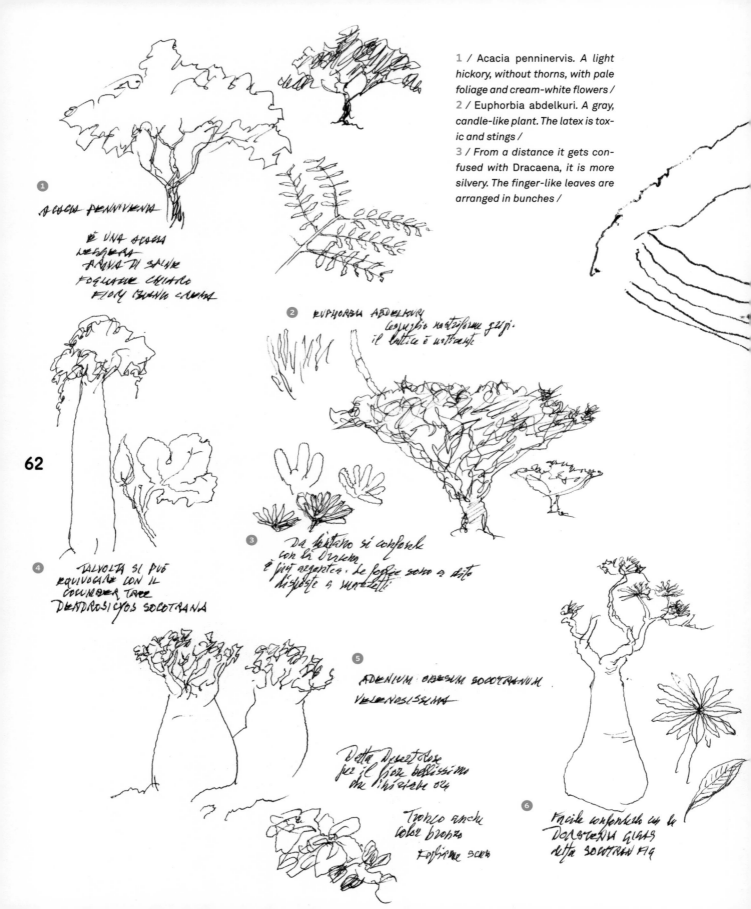

1 / Acacia penninervis. *A light hickory, without thorns, with pale foliage and cream-white flowers* /

2 / Euphorbia abdelkuri. *A gray, candle-like plant. The latex is toxic and stings* /

3 / *From a distance it gets confused with Dracaena, it is more silvery. The finger-like leaves are arranged in bunches* /

62

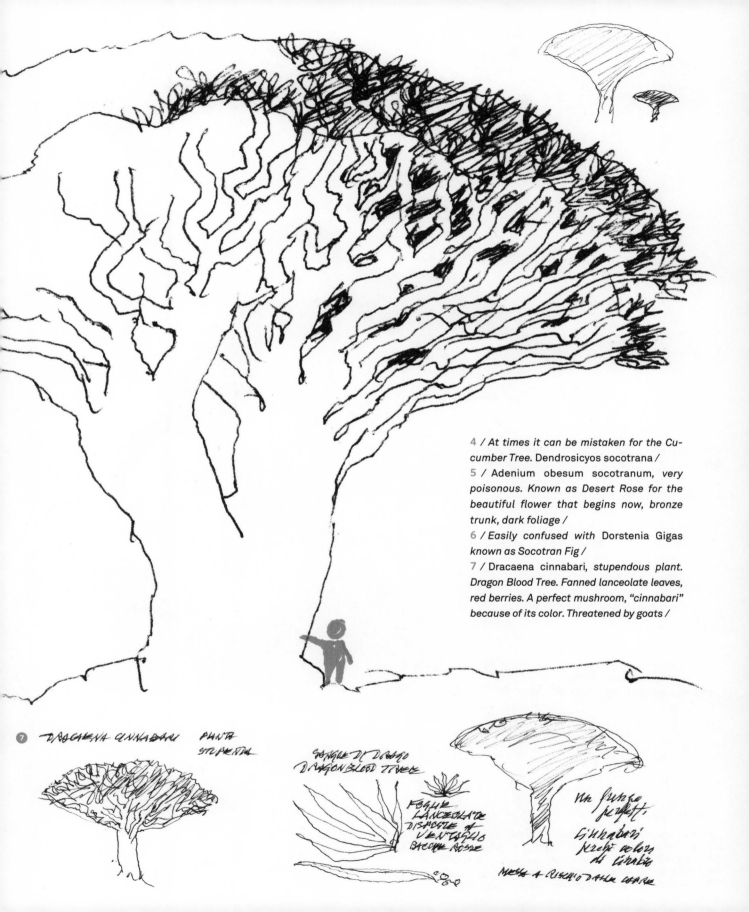

4 / At times it can be mistaken for the Cucumber Tree. Dendrosicyos socotrana /

5 / Adenium obesum socotranum, *very poisonous. Known as Desert Rose for the beautiful flower that begins now, bronze trunk, dark foliage /*

6 / *Easily confused with Dorstenia Gigas known as Socotran Fig /*

7 / Dracaena cinnabari, *stupendous plant. Dragon Blood Tree. Fanned lanceolate leaves, red berries. A perfect mushroom, "cinnabari" because of its color. Threatened by goats /*

1 L'OCCHIO DEL FALCO

2 MA LO STARLING È UNO STORNO? E LO SPARROW È IL PASSERO? E LO STRIKE SARÀ UNO SCRICCIOLO?

3 GRANDI GAMBALUNGA MALINCONICI E SOLITARI SULLA BATTIGIA IN ATTESA DI GRANCHIOLINI

4 BUFFI UCCELLI PICCOLISSIMI CON LA TESTA ZEBRATA

5 NEPHRON PERCNOPTERUS AVVOLTOIO EGIZIANO ONNIPRESENTE

6 PETTIROSSO O GARDELLINO? ONICHOGNATUS FRATER UNO STORNO SOCOTRANO

NOI SIAMO QUI LA FEMMINA HA TESTA E COLLO GRIGI ELEGANTISSIMA IL MASCHIO È TUTTO NERO

64

7 SIA IL MASCHIO SIA LA FEMMINA HANNO L'INTERNO DELLE ALI ROSSO

8 30 DIC. 2006
SIAMO SCAPPATI DAI MARGINI DEL CAMPO FISSO ANDANDO A PIANTARE LA TENDA SOTTO QUEI GROSSI ROCCIONE COLOR RUGGINE. LÀ DOVE TERMINA LA LAGUNA SONO ARRIVATI, STANOTTE, UNDICI GRUPPI DI AVVENTURE NEL MONDO. ISOLA DESERTA - ADDIO -

Sketch, Think, Draw.

1 / *Eye of the falcon* /
2 / *But is the starling a storno? And is the sparrow a passero? And is the shrike a scricciolo?* /
3 / *Big melancholy solitary longlegs on the shore in search of little crabs* /
4 / *Funny very small birds with zebra-striped heads* /
5 / *Neophron percnopterus, the omnipresent Egyptian vulture* /
6 / *Robin or blackcap? Onychognathus frater. A Socotra starling, the female has very elegant gray head and neck, the male is all black* /
7 / *Both male and female have red under their wings* /
8 / *We fled from the boundaries of the camp and pitched our tent under that big rust-colored stone, at the end of the lagoon. Eleven Avventure nel mondo groups arrived this evening... goodbye desert island!* /

66

67

❝ The mind and the eye see things, understand them, change them, deform them, all very quickly, and the hand has to be seamlessly bonded to the thought. That mark might seem like a little "scribble," but in that moment, drawn in that way, it is useful. **❞**

69

/ From Hosteria Las Torres, *you see the* Torres del Paine *more or less like this. What strikes you most, besides the imposing massif, is the gritty look of the Torres that seem to almost suddenly rise from a barren plain with low hills coated with vague vegetation. The aggressive look comes from these black patches, these big rocks, that rise beyond the vertical walls of ice. Unreachable. Forbidding. Even provocative /*

Giancarlo Iliprandi

Aiguille Noire de Peuterey, Mont Blanc

Sketch, Think, Draw.

Aiguille Noire de Peuterey

Giancarlo Iliprandi

Aiguille Noire de Peuterey, Mont Blanc

Dent du Géant

#2

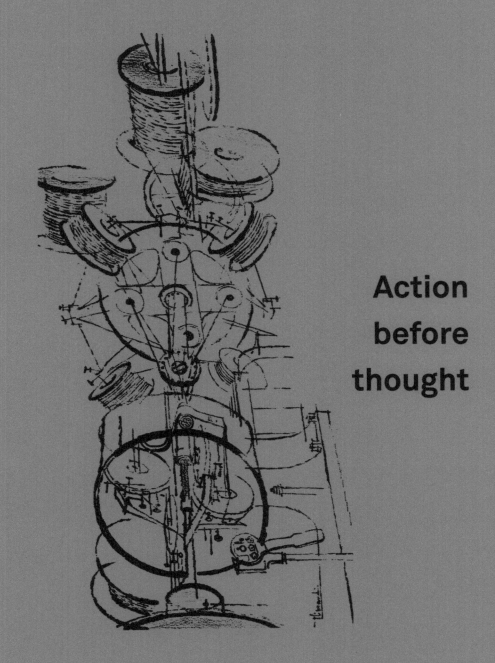

Action
before
thought

Action before thought

In all of Iliprandi's graphic work, there is a strong element of drawing. Unlike many other Italian graphic designers of his generation, who came from the world of product design, architecture or printing, Iliprandi studied painting and scenography at the Fine Arts Academy of Brera. He lived his formative years in reverse disrupting traditional design processes: it is the gesture, even in its unpredictable imprecision, that becomes the central focus of his work.

In his archives, there are rigid, gridded layouts mixed, and often overlapping, with freehand drawings. "The practice of looking at Goya's painting of the firing squad, or *Guernica* by Picasso, or Piero della Francesca with the hanging egg creates a memory bank. These *banked images*, no matter where you go or what you see, they affect your way of drawing without a conscious awareness."

"Repeating the same gesture over and over, like a Samurai who practices with his sword all day, at a certain point the gesture becomes instinctive, it's inside of you!

Studies for the layout, Ex Oriente, book by Lanfranco Colombo, 1963

80

It becomes part of your code. And this also happens when the action has been nurtured, time and time again, in thought. Action before thought.

There can be stimuli of different kinds: various qualities of paper, different pens, sunlight or the lack of sunlight … there are so many variables. Yet, in that moment you don't pause to think, in that moment, you only make the drawing. Action is what counts. Thoughts about how you made it will come, perhaps, but only later."

Grid studies, Modulo typeface, Nebiolo, 1976

81

It is not just a question of using drawing in a graphic design context, but a much deeper question of method. The pursuit of quality at the level of the line, even before one turns to the quality of the design itself, has to do with the need for synthesis and simplicity. While many artists seek this synthesis in the perfection of geometry and mathematics, Iliprandi shows us that it is more a humanistic than a scientific process: "When you start to think/sketch, the creative moment is very short, it's the

IMPUNTURA
A SEI MILLIMETRI

CUCITURE
RIMBOCCLATE

COLLO
CLASSICO
A DOPPIO
USO

MARTINGALA
TESA

AMPIO
SFONDO
PIEGA

TASCHE CON
ALETTA E
PROFILO

LINEA
A VITA

MODELLO
HSP 66

o uso classico - tasche con alette e pro-
/3 bottoni/martingala tesa - cuciture
dietro - impuntura a mm. 8 al collo,

ue à double usage - poches à rabats -
utons/martingale - coutures rabattues
piqûre à 8 mm. au col, au devant, aux

le-purpose traditional collar - flapped
k with cannon / 3 buttons / stretched
sleeves, at the sides, at the back center
flaps - marked waist-line. *********

klassischer Kragen, der offen un ge-
nd Nähten - 2 Knöpfe an der Ärmel-
leiste - Nähte an den Schultern, Är-
8 mm Abstand am Kragen, vorne, an

Hitman catalogue, 1965

beginning. Again, action comes before thought—you pull out what you have inside.

A mark has its own shorthand: not only when you draw birds, but also when you design a trademark or the layout of a page. The mind and the eye see things, understand them, change them, deform them, all very quickly, and the hand has to be seamlessly bonded to the thought. As Kandinsky said, the point is the beginning of a dialogue between you and the blank page. You are in front of the blank page and there is silence, but then that point interrupts the silence, and a dialogue begins."

One wonders who the parties in this dialogue are. In the travel drawings, it is clearly a three-way conversation between what is seen, the artist, and the page. When a project has been commissioned, the third party is not what is there in front of the artist, but instead the brief submitted by the client.

The gesture is no longer the mechanical movement of leaving a mark; it is finding a design solution. Not just the hand, but the mind, too, has to be fast.

Iliprandi explained this to me straightforwardly and effectively, as a good draftsman would: "When they tell you 'it would be nice to do a book for Moleskine,' it's not that now, knowing you have to make a book, you hold this information in until you get to the studio, and out of nothing turn on the light and say: 'Well, now I'll do the book for Moleskine.' During the day you will already

83

have had little flashes of intuition, in which you might glimpse the directions to develop. Maybe you have even had a few flashes of, 'Oh God, I have to make a book, what am I going to do?' You must therefore train yourself to get used to making decisions when you're doing a project on commission—train yourself by taking on a lot of work, and by looking at the work of those around you. Going to see Goya is like a voyage, is like going to the desert. You must store up a great number of solutions and models, to be able to then rework them at the right time."

Then comes the method and rigor of a profession with its own set of rules. To lay out a book, for example, you have to think about the division of space on the page, about the margins, the format, etc. Therefore you need a method. Iliprandi's work in this book, respecting these rules, is always combined with something that is both poised and disorderly, almost impertinent, just like Iliprandi himself. The courage to move beyond frameworks, so evident in different forms throughout Iliprandi's career, is thanks to the knowledge of those very frameworks and the confidence that comes with being able to control them.

costrizione non è soluzione

" The mark has many applications:
it can be precise, technical, boring ...
But the mark also has its own shorthand,
a rapid shorthand, which is important:
not only when you draw birds, but also
when you design a trademark
or the layout of a page. "

Studies, *Serigrafia* magazine, 1975

Illustration for the article *Sugli sci*, written by *Gianbruno*,
the pseudonym of Giancarlo Iliprandi and Bruno Vergot-
tini. These are the hats of friends who skied with him.
Esquire & Derby magazine #11-12, 1977

SCE - SCE

LO PASSI CON UN
CAPO SULLA TESTA
E LO TIENI
TRA I DENTI

COMPERI
IL TESSUTO
A METRAGGIO

DPPURE LO
BUTTI SULLA
SPALLA
DPPOSTA

CON QUELLO CHE
OVANRA FAI UN
SALAMOTTO
ATTORCIGLIATO
O QUASI MORBIDO

POI LO GIRI
SOPRA LA
FRONTE

FINCHÉ NON
SEI TUTTO
AVVOLTO

COSI

COSI

COSI

SECONDO IL FREDDO IL SOLE L'ESTRO LA VOGLIA

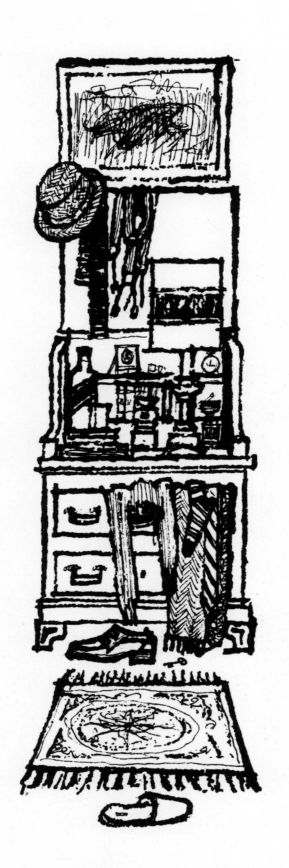

SELEZIONE ABBIGLIAMENTO SPORTIVO

Un gruppo di stilisti ha costruito e coordinato uno shop di abbigliamento sportivo che la Rinascente presenta dal 13 al 27 ottobre. ❧ Capitolo fondamentale i completi « spezzati »: le giacche di Harry's tweed, di velluto a coste e di loden, i blazer blu, tutti i pantaloni che le completano. ❧ Un gruppo importante è rappresentato dalle cravatte di lana, di foulard, regimental e dalle scarpe inglesi, nel cuoio e nei colori tradizionali. ❧ I pullovers di cammello, di lambswool e di cachemire costituiscono da soli una piccola mostra. ❧ La Rinascente con questa prima presentazione dà il via ad un programma vastissimo che vedrà per tutto il 1963 ❧ i settori dell'abbigliamento maschile impegnati in una successione di avvenimenti promozionali. ❧ ❧ ❧

la Rinascente
Piazza Fiume   Piazza Colonna

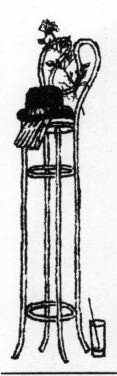

93

LA SERA VESTIRSI DA SERA

Dal 3 novembre rassegna dell'abito elegante da pomeriggio e da sera in tutte le sue componenti. ❧ L'argomento di maggior interesse è il cappotto blu. ❧ Lo accompagnano gli abiti interi da pranzo, completati da tutti gli accessori: ❧ scarpe di vitello nero, guanti di gazzella e di nappa, camicie, cravatte a pois e a righe, ❧ calze di seta e di filo, cinture di foca e di vitello opaco. ❧ Per la prima volta, gli smoking, e le camicie esatte pieghettate, ❧ le fasce alte da mettere in vita, le scarpe di vernice, i gemelli in pietra dura. ❧ ❧ ❧ ❧ ❧

la Rinascente
Roma Piazza Fiume Piazza Colonna

Still Lifes, newspapers advertising for *La Rinascente*, 1965

Drawings for the exhibition *I promessi sposi*, Lecco, 2001

The characters are based on Spanish painters of the 17th century.
Left to right / Francisco de Zurbarán, Diego Velázquez and Juan Ricci

ei un amico
el Museo
Poldi Pezzoli?

MOLTO LIBERAMENTE
D'APRÈS VAN DYCK
PER SERIGRAFIA
ILIPRANDI. 76

Cover *Molto liberamente d'apres Van Dyck*, *Serigrafia* magazine, 1976

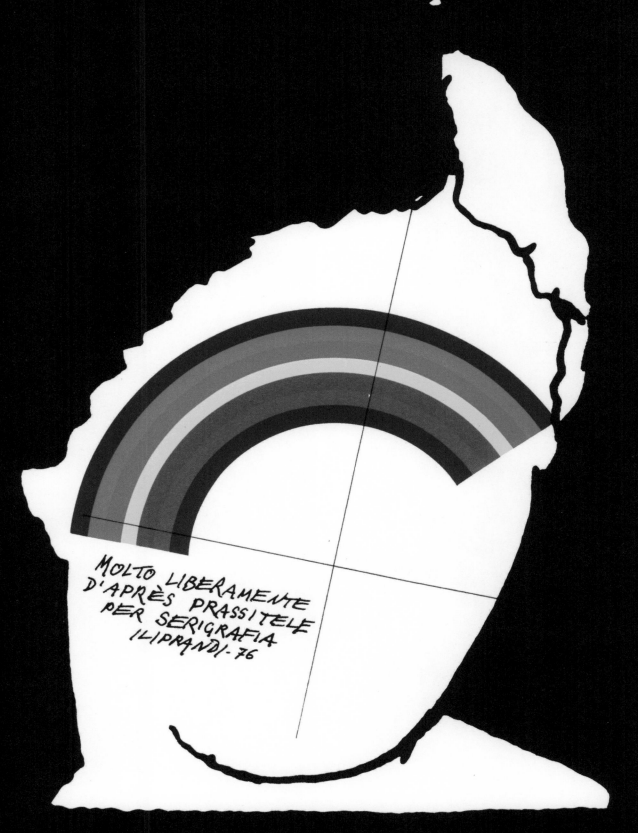

Cover *Molto liberamente d'apres Prassitele*, Serigrafia magazine, 1976

Studies and poster *10° Autunno musicale napoletano*, 1967

X autunno musicale napoletano

Rai Radiotelevisione Italiana / Azienda Autonoma di Soggiorno Cura e Turismo di Napoli / Associazione Alessandro Scarlatti di Napoli

Napoli 14/29 Ottobre / Auditorium della RAI / Teatro di Corte del Palazzo Reale di Napoli

" The medium
is fundamental.
It is very important
to have paper I can
trust, because being
able to make a good
mark depends on
the paper. **"**

Drawings from *Buongiorno Signor Doré*,
ILDE, Festival of Artist's Books and
Small Editions, Barcelona, 2011

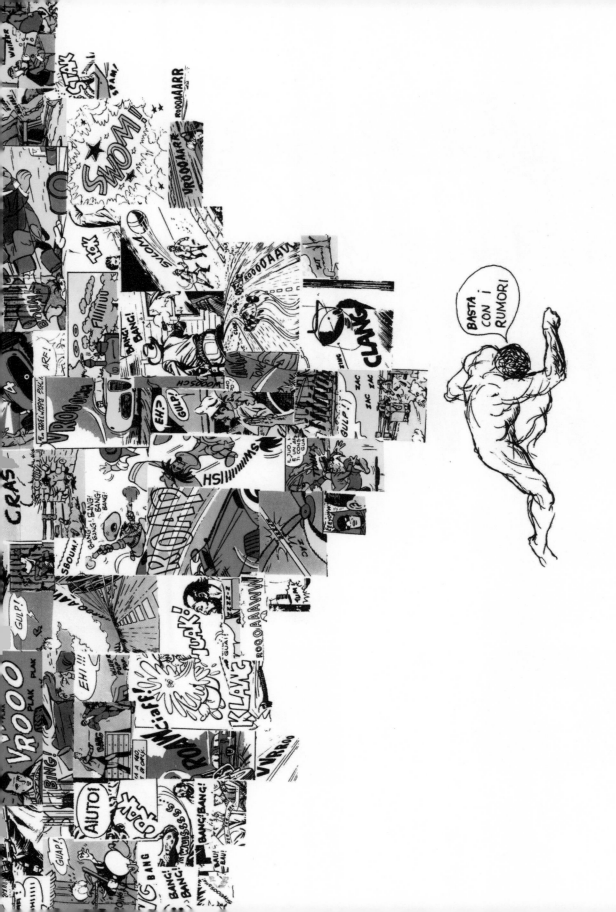

Poster *Basta con i rumori!* / Enough noise! /, *Imago* magazine #8, 1965

Drawings on rice paper,
exhibition at Libreria del
Salto, Milan, 1961

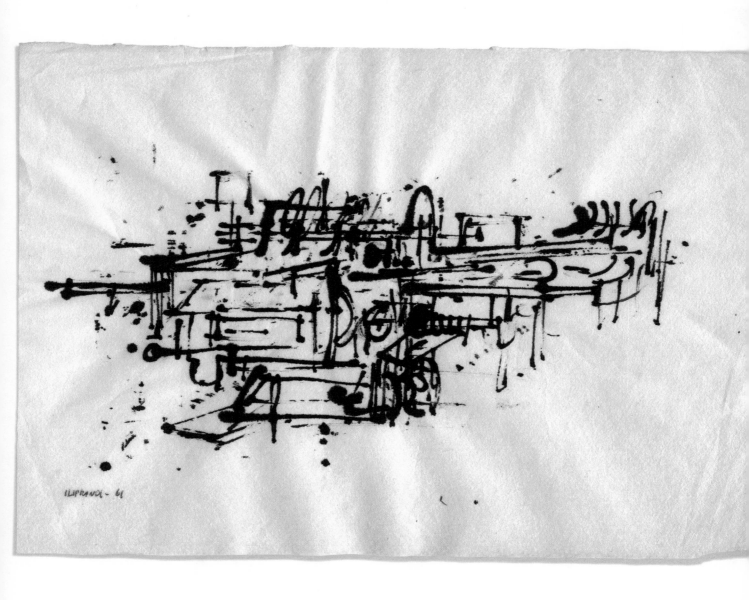

Printing press, ink on rice paper, 1961

Printing press, ink on rice paper, 1961

Giancarlo Iliprandi

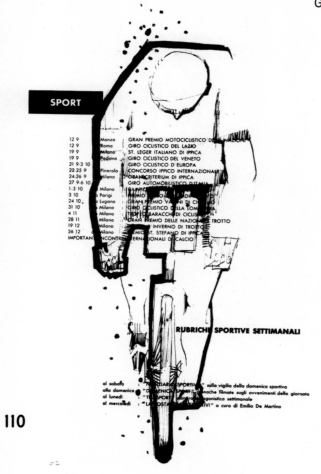

on this page / **Drawings for *RAI***, exhibit designed by Achille and Pier Giacomo Castiglioni, 1954

on the facing page / **Drawing for *Istituto Italiano del Marchio di Qualità***, exhibit designed by Achille and Pier Giacomo Castiglioni, 1957

110

☆ L'Istituto Italiano del Marchio esegue i controlli che voi non potreste eseguire ☆ fa ciò che voi non potreste fare ☆ lo fa nel vostro interesse.

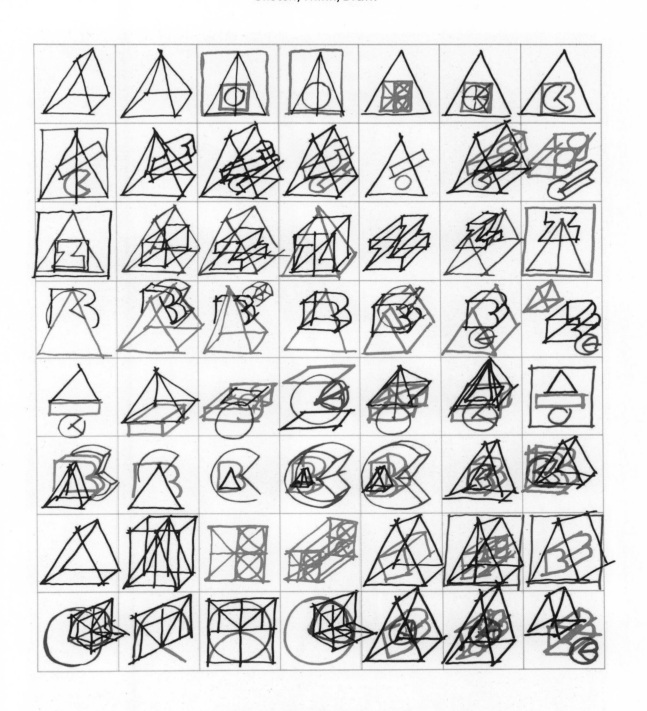

113

left / **Poster *Un po' di Giappone a Milano* /
A bit of Japan in Milan /**, *Arflex*, 1974

above / **Studies for *Alfabeta* large screen
prints**, *Nava*, 1977

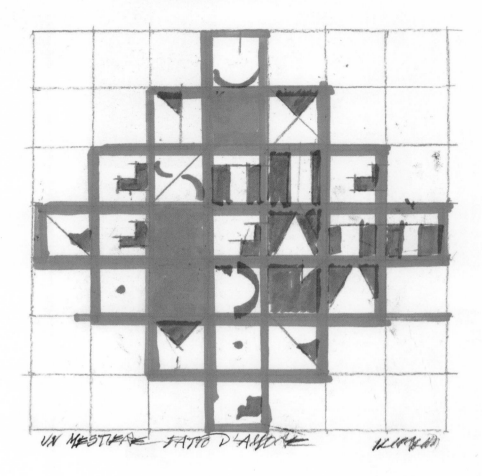

UN MESTIERE FATTO D'AMORE

/ A craft made of love /

“ To write and to draw
—it's the same thing. Writing, too,
is a manual gesture that begins in
thought and is then put to paper. I like
to look at certain written pages—even
badly written ones—because they are
always drawings: a way of marking
one's territory, just as animals do. ”

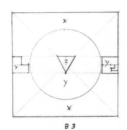

B 3

X ROSSO MATTONE RUSSINE
Y ROSA
Z ARANCIO

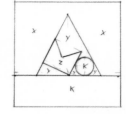

A 1

X GIALLO TRICROMIA
Y SIENA NATURALE OCRA
K OMBRA NATURALE
Z OMBRA BRUCIATA < NATURALE + VERDE

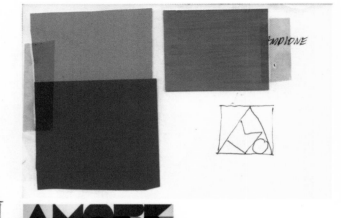

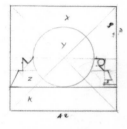

A 2

X BLU COBALTO+PRUSSIA •
Y TURCHESE + VERDE
Z VERDE PINO SCURO
K VERDE TRICROMIA •

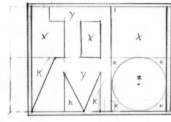

X BLU COBALTO
Y GRIGIO CHIARO
K VERDE PALLIDO
Z GRIGIO SCURO

116

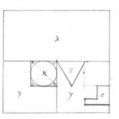

B 1

X SIENA NATURALE OCRA 29
Y SIENA BRUCIATA 68.

B 2

X COBALTO SCURO
Y VERDE PINO SCURO
Z VERDE BIGLIARDO • INTENSO UN PO' DI BLU
K GIALLO TRICROMIA

GRIGIO CHIARO
GRIGIO SCURO
ROSA
BRUNO

ROSA PIÙ SCURO
DI QUELLO DEL BOZZETTO

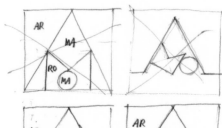

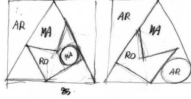

X BLU COBALTO
Y GRIGIO CHIARO
Z VERDE BIANCO
O GRIGIO SCURO
K VERDE PALLIDO

GRIGIO
CHIARO

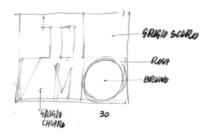

GRIGIO SCURO
ROSA
BRUNO

30

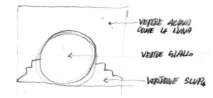

VERDE ACQUA
COME LA LUNA
VERDE GIALLO
VERDE SCURO

on this page / Studies for Alfabeta large screen prints, Nava, 1977 / on the facing page / Advertising for Forma typeface, Nebiolo, 1968

/ FORMA harmonic FORMA cyclical FORMA rhythmical FORMA static FORMA dynamic FORMA full FORMA round FORMA constant FORMA recurring FORMA usual FORMA new FORMA complete FORMA open FORMA concluded FORMA traced FORMA sought FORMA invented FORMA ideal FORMA total FORMA modern FORMA timely FORMA printed FORMA spatial FORMA pure FORMA autonomous FORMA block FORMA formal FORMA decisive FORMA precise FORMA NEBIOLO /

FORMA armonica FORMA ciclica FORMA ritmica FORM
A statica FORMA dinamica FORMA piena FORMA tonda
FORMA costante FORMA ricorrente FORMA consueta F
ORMA nuova FORMA compiuta FORMA aperta FORMA
conclusa FORMA tracciata FORMA cercata FORMA ide
ata FORMA ideale FORMA totale FORMA moderna FOR
MA attuale FORMA stampata FORMA spaziale FORMA
pura FORMA autonoma FORMA cubitale FORMA forma
le FORMA decisa FORMA precisa **FORMA NEBIOLO**

tipo
cromo

/ Lettering is an art as ancient as man /

above / **Study for an alphabet of lines and dots,**
Serigrafia magazine, 1980

right / **Cover Arcobaleno, Molto liberamente d'après
Iliprandi /Rainbow/,** *Serigrafia* magazine, 1976

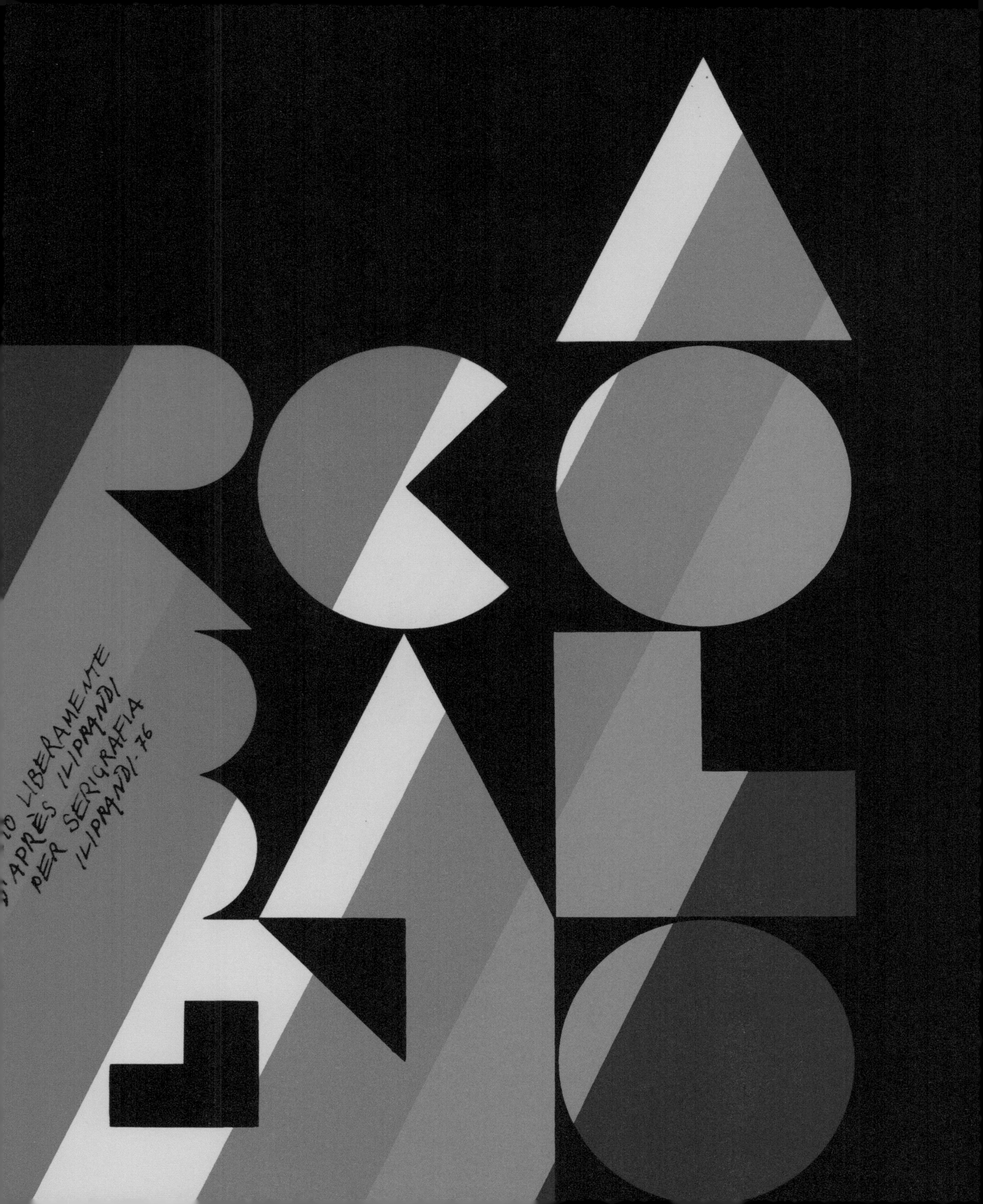

PROBAL TO

10 LIBERAMENTE
D'APRÈS ILIPRANDI
PER SERIGRAFIA
ILIPRANDI-76

COSI MARGINE DI 7 Cm

RIPRESA — 1. COPIA 20 X 20 — ₣ 2 COPIE 13 X 18.

above / **Preparatory drawing for the contributors'
page**, *Sci Nautico* magazine

right / **Cover**, *Serigrafia* magazine, 1989

Norcia, piccola Città d' Itallia nell'Umbria, nel Ducatto di Spoletto. Abbenchè soggetta alla santa Sedde, forma nondimeno una specie di Repubblica, ed elegge quattro Maestratti. San Benedetto naccue in questa Città, e vi ebber pure i loro natali Giambatt. Lalli,

/ We are so accustomed to playing with the letters of our alphabet that we can afford to play, with commentary, even with the genius of Giambattista Bodoni, here on a page of the Manuale Tipografico, Parma 1788, two centuries ago, may that good soul forgive modern graphics when it uses the character as a pretext /

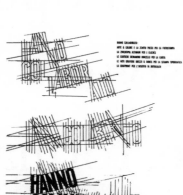

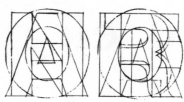

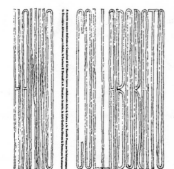

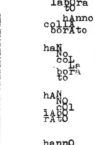

> **When you begin to design, action comes before thought because you extrapolate from everything you have stored up over time.**

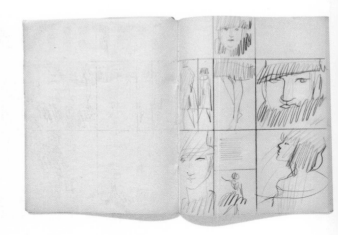

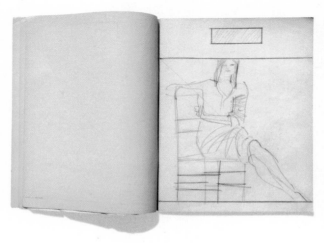

Sketch, Think, Draw.

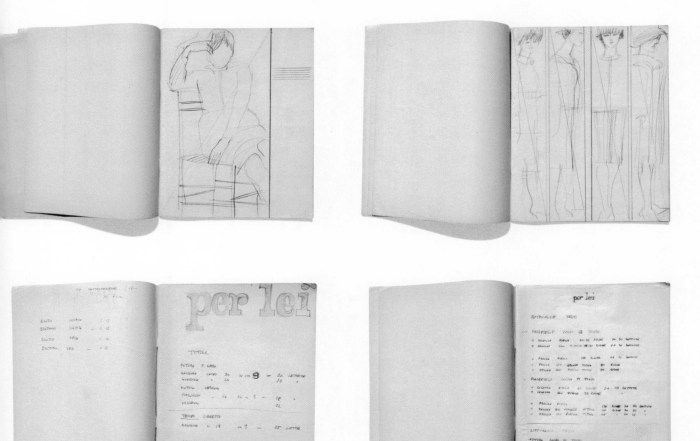

Studies, women's fashion catalogue
for *La Rinascente,* 1960s

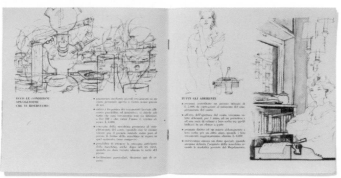

Booklet *Lettera 22, Lettera allo studente / Lettera 22, Letter to the student /*, Olivetti, 1959

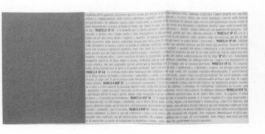

Hitman catalogue, winter collection, 1965

Drawing for *Organizzazione Pubblicitaria Italiana*, booklet design by Albe Steiner, 1957

Sketch, Think, Draw.

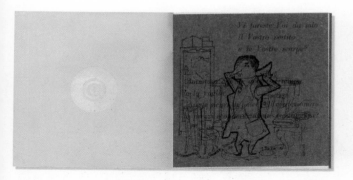

/ Would you make your clothing or your shoes for yourself?
Even if you had the time and the desire to do so, would you
be sure you could make them at an advantageous price? /

/ Would you rely on your trusted mechanic to simultaneously
take care of your automobile, your watch and your radio? /

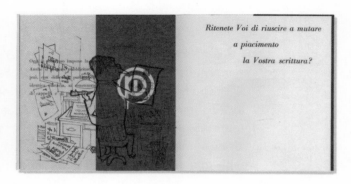

/ Do you think you can change your writing at will? /

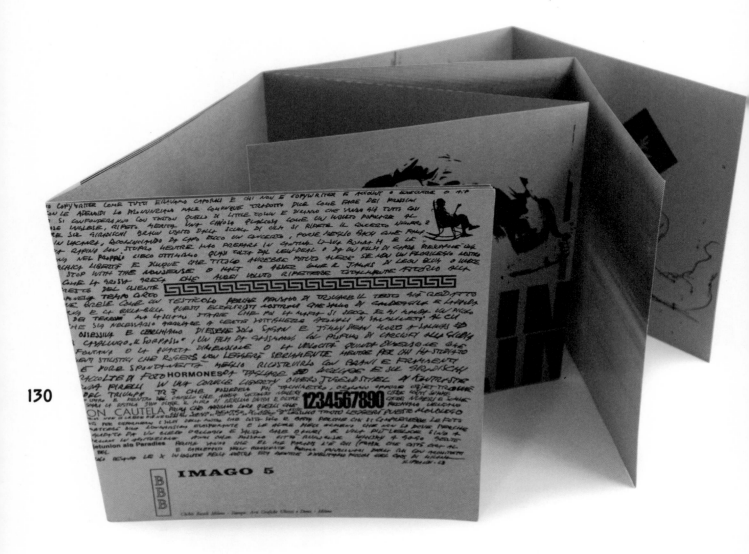

❝ No Ladies and Gentlmen IMAGO is indeed spontaneity and it would be better reconstruct it with bits and fragments not like a DADA print but rather as a composition by Rauschenberg or Jasper Johns with items which have already lived a life of their own and can bring some emotion so here I am at last leafing through weekly magazines portfolios of old drawings and collections of photographs to cut and paste ... **❞**

Sketch, Think, Draw.

Imago **magazine #5,** 1965

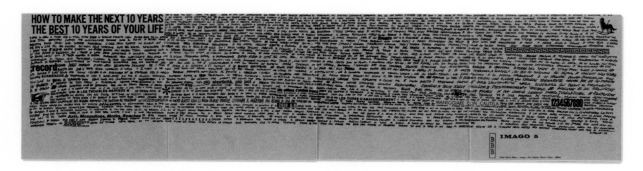

venerdì 7 giugno

77

8

9 UMANITARIA

10 SHOVENAGE — TEL RUFFINI

UBEZZI K. DOMES

11 CR

APP. BALLO ? TEMPORIUM

12

TEL TRECCANI

13 MADERNA

ALBE 34-20-27

14 69-95 CARLO ERBA (FOTO

Ronato WTENA 262 SN)

15

16 LIBIS & ARDEN. J&R - in WINTER

17 TEL MONECA WAISL - CROCENZI

18 SCIMUTICO NO 36 1/2

GRAFFPRINT (CARROZZERIA SOFFRITTI)

19 PASSOLI PER IMAGO TEL 289-5741

20 JIMORO — TEL SPAZIO

UMANITARIA VETRINE — TE.

Sketch, Think, Draw.

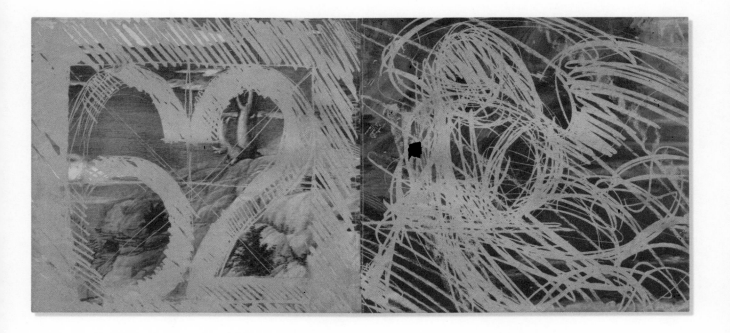

Sci Nautico **magazine's Holiday special,** printed in gold on discarded advance sheets, 1962

#3

Who is
Giancarlo
Iliprandi

Who is Giancarlo Iliprandi

I began drawing rather late, when I was almost twenty years old. The political situation at the time had forced me into hiding. I copied classic illustrations I found in the books my father collected. Before, I had only kept school notebooks, where I clumsily imitated the authors of the satirical newspaper *Bertoldo*. But I had always written things; I kept journals, even when I was a child. Those pages, in any case, remained a way of communicating. Probably the task for which I'm best suited. I decided to learn to draw, and I chose the Brera Fine Arts Academy in Milan. I was a student there; I enrolled first as a painter, then studied as a set designer (1945-53). After graduating, I was seduced by graphic design, which wasn't taught in those days, and began studying it on my own. My last show of paintings was a solo effort at Galleria dell'Ariete in 1957.

In 1960 I was offered a position, teaching a famous course for assistant graphic designers at Società Umanitaria. To teach, I had to study, especially typography.

After that I no longer drew for the pleasure of drawing, though I often used drawing in my visual communication projects.

The drawings I did throughout the 1960s, 1970s and 1980s, like the photographs, were meant as communicative aids. These drawings were never an end unto themselves, much less works that could qualify as "art." In 1988 I went to the Sahara for the first time, and I was fascinated by the spaces and personalities I encountered along the way. In 1989 I brought some colored pencils with me to document the atmosphere I found myself confronted with. Modest drawings. But it wasn't until the 1990s that I discovered the convenience of watercolors—and rediscovered the pleasure of putting marks on paper, just for the sake of doing it.

Now when I look back, in my mind, I come across bundles of drawings, piles of notebooks. On which, for better or worse, I have left evidence of my journey. Maybe, if I stop to think about it, more than anything else they are complicit in moments of peace achieved by moving the hand, almost automatically.

Drawing is a wonderful medicine. It spoils you without you realizing it. It helps you enter into the landscape by deepening your point of view. It helps reveal people, as you try to grasp their hidden lives. Chasing fragments, details, sketches, before they escape from your thoughts.

Giancarlo Iliprandi

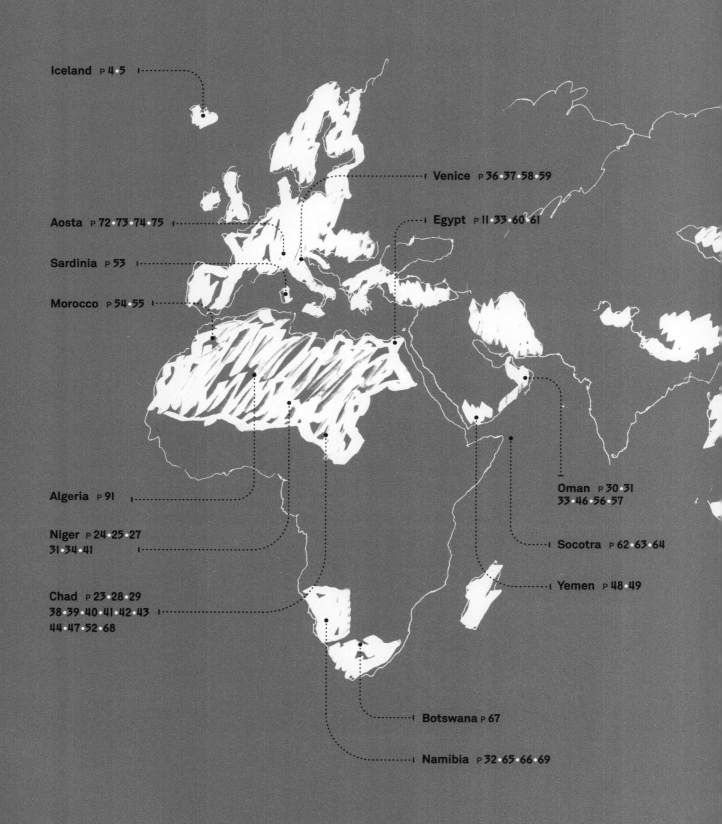

#4 geographical index